Our Hearts Are Restless

Our Hearts Are Restless

The Prayer of St. Augustine

F. J. SHEED

Photographs by Catharine Hughes

A CROSSROAD BOOK
THE SEABURY PRESS · NEW YORK

The Seabury Press
815 Second Avenue
New York, N.Y. 10017

Library of Congress Catalog Card Number: 76-20197
ISBN: 0-8164-2127-7

INTRODUCTION

Our hearts are restless till they rest in You.

Augustine has this at the beginning of his *Confessions*. With it any study of his prayers must begin, for all of them are concerned without restlessness or its quieting.

Two of them are famous everywhere:

Lord, give me chastity, but not yet!

and

Late have I loved You, Beauty so ancient and so new.

The prayers he prayed in his progress from the first to the second, and the prayers which flowed out of the second, are what this small book is about.

He tells it all in dazzling detail in the *Confessions,* written when he was in his middle forties, after eight or nine years of priesthood, in his first years as bishop. No bishop has ever examined his conscience in public so shamelessly.

About this he had no choice, for he was examining himself under the gaze of God.

In Your presence I am telling it to . . . the race of men, or rather to that small part of the human race which may come upon these writings. And to what purpose? That I and they may realize out of what depths we can rise to You.

But again and again we find him forgetting his readers and telling his story direct to God. "It is only for Your glory that I confess to you all my ingloriousness." That sentence was framed by the Professor of Rhetoric that he had once been. But what it was saying was not rhetoric. He had the same two "luminous certainties" as Newman fifteen centuries later—God and himself. Neither man meant that nothing else existed for him, but only that of nothing else was he so continuously, blindingly, aware. One may doubt if Augustine ever lost the awareness of God, even in the moment of the sexual climax he so endlessly sought and endlessly found—once, so he tells us, in church while Mass was being offered. The awareness must have been rather complicating.

In old age, he remembers that he read the *Confessions* again—with emotion. I wonder if anyone has ever read them unmoved.

POSTSCRIPT

Bracketed references are from my own translation of Augustine's *Confessions,* from which come nearly all of the prayers quoted. I should explain that in translating him I made no attempt to match his magnificence. He writes at times with molten lava. I lack lava. I hope my Englishing of his prayers brings out the meaning, but I miss the lava.

MAN OF TWO PASSIONS

I

Augustine was born in North Africa in 353. His birth-town was Tagaste, of which his father, Patricius, was a decurion, which meant that he was above the poverty line, though perhaps not enough for comfort: he was not yet a Christian but was to become one. His mother Monica (which she would have spelled Monnica) Augustine has made world famous, hundreds of churches named after her, thousands of women, a beach in California: in the sixteenth century a Spanish priest saw a spring there which in its exuberance reminded him of Monica's weeping as she prayed for her son's conversion.

The Augustine we know was a man of two passions, passion for sex, passion for truth, both at white-heat—each indeed at an intensity beyond that of most of the specialists in one or the other.

The first to emerge was lust of the flesh. He was already something of a practitioner of sex while still a schoolboy. Patricius managed to raise the money to send him a couple of hundred miles off to Carthage to complete his study of Rhetoric. There "a cauldron of illicit loves leapt and boiled about me." Back in Tagaste his mother Monica had urged him not to sin with women, especially with married women. "I would have blushed to obey." Indeed he tells us, "I was ashamed among the other youths that my viciousness was less than theirs; I heard them boasting of their exploits, and the viler the exploits the louder the boasting; and I set about the same exploits not only for the pleasure of the act but for the pleasure of the boasting." At no point, one observes, does Augustine show any consciousness of what the viler of the exploits may have meant to the women. He goes on, "I grew in vice through desire of praise; and when I lacked opportunity to equal others in vice, I invented things I had not done."

Pause upon Monica. Her devotion to her son has become a legend, but one gets the impression that her judgment was nearly always bad, verging at one point near the end on the sheerly idiotic. She adored him. Did he return her adoration in equal measure? One can but guess. What is certain is that it is hard to think of anything he did because she wanted it. Her prayers and tears may well have had the effect on God that Augustine says they had; they seem to have had no clearly traceable effect on her son. But then, as Augustine would have known, the effect on God is what matters: "She brought me forth—in the flesh to this temporal light, in her heart to life eternal."

Certainly it was not to please her that he took a mistress. There is no sentiment in his first mention of this girl whose name he never tells us. "I took one woman, not joined to me in lawful marriage, but one whom wandering lust and no particular judgment had brought my way. Yet I had but that one woman and I was faithful to her. With her I learnt by experience what a gulf there is between the restraint of the marriage covenant entered into for the sake of

children and the mere bargain of a lustful love, where if children come they come unwanted—though when they are born they compel our love.''

A son was born. Augustine called him Adeodatus—God-given —and adored him. The union lasted fifteen years. Does "faithful" mean that he had no more casual embracings for all those years? At a time when even respectable married men—like Augustine's father —had them as a matter of course, it seems improbable. To a man as fascinating as Augustine plenty of women must have offered themselves, and the man he has been describing was not likely to have refused them. "Faithful," I think, means that she was the undisputed woman in residence, with as much fidelity as the average wife could expect. One thinks of Ernest Dowson's "I have been faithful to thee, Cynara, in my fashion."

Their fifteen years together came to a miserable end. To the men of that day it would probably have seemed wholly normal: you take a concubine for your convenience, you send her away for your convenience—doubtless with enough money to bridge the time of her unemployment. But in so many ways Augustine was not a man of that day, or indeed of any day: in any day he would have been unique. A dozen years later he told the story in the *Confessions*. By that time anyhow he must have felt himself detestable, treating a human being as a mere object, and he must have known how detestable he must look to his Christian readers.

He was writing with no concern about man's scorn, he says, his sole concern was God's mercy. He was showing God and man his ingloriousness, and here was its lowest depth. His other sins were in the heat of the blood, this was cold-blooded—with the coldness of a different heat; ''I was hot for honors, money, marriage.'' A provincial governorship, like Pontius Pilate's, was a possibility. ''I could marry a wife with some little money of her own, so that she would not increase my expenditure.''

His mother set about getting him properly married. A girl was asked for and promised. Here comes the point which sets us wondering about Monica's sanity—the girl was two years under the legal age for marriage. Augustine agreed to wait. But he couldn't wait. He took another mistress, ''not of course as a wife.''

The first one had been thrown out—''torn from my side'' is his phrase, torn from her son's side too. She went home to Africa, swearing that she would never know another man—but ''I, for all my manhood, could not imitate her resolve.''

For the only time, he tells what she and the union we have heard him call ''the mere bargain of a lustful love'' had really meant to him: ''My heart, in which she had made her own special place, was broken, wounded, bled. The wound did not heal. For there was first a burning and bitter grief. After that it festered, and as the pain grew duller, it grew only more hopeless.''

It was in another context that he cried: ''Who can unravel this complex and twisted knottedness?'' Let us try unravelling this one. Monica may have thought Augustine would stay chaste for two years. Augustine of course knew he couldn't. Why did he agree? He tells us when he talks of the next mistress—''I didn't want marriage but lust.''

What he meant by lust we get in the last struggle before he gave sexual union up forever (8.11). His old lusts ''plucking at his garment of flesh''—murmured ''Shall this and that not be allowed you, now or forever?'' They were not saying ''this and that'' *(hoc et illud)* of course: he writes it so for decency's sake. But he tells us of "the vileness and uncleanness" the words covered—not straight sexual intercourse but the obscene variations and perversions by which the promiscuous try to disguise the plain emptiness the act always comes to have when there is only linking of bodies and no union of persons.

The act is not in itself obscene. God did not make the continuance of the race depend on an obscenity. But the act itself was not what Augustine wanted; he wanted these extras, the sort of thing which he could demand of a mistress but not so surely of a wife, which in any event he should not have as a Christian. I cannot of course guarantee this interpretation of *hoc et illud*. But at least it would explain the puzzling fact that he assumed that baptism meant the end of sexual activity. I have seen no other explanation—for at that time, and for years after, he had no thought of becoming a priest. If I am right, then he knew—as Monica did not—that as a Christian celibacy was the only safe way for him. That "cauldron of illicit loves" which "leapt and boiled" about him in Carthage need not have been mere rhetoric. In a Mediterranean seaport every sexual eccentricity from Scandinavia to Syria and the Black Sea would have been known and catered to.

It is interesting that Augustine manages to convey his horror at "this and that" without giving a hint as to what it might have been. A bookseller once advertised the *Confessions* (in my translation) as "sex-drenched." He was misleading his customers. No one will learn from him anything about sex that he does not already know. Its power and the uncleanness it can have, Augustine conveys not by spreading himself on its detail but by giving us himself, his memory scarred with it, his whole being scarred.

II

All this while, the other passion, for truth, had been growing. It was less spectacular, outwardly at least, but it never lost its grip on him and in the end it was decisive.

It began, to me incredibly, with his reading of "a book of one Cicero," when he was eighteen. The book was the *Hortensius,* now lost, surviving only in quotations. "It changed the direction of my mind, altered my prayers, gave me a new purpose. . . . With an incredible intensity of desire I began to long after immortal wisdom. I had begun that journey upward by which I was to return to You." (3.4).

The first effect was *not* to lead him to the Scriptures—he "had not the mind to penetrate into their depths" and the writing in them was not to be compared with Cicero's! Instead he joined the Manichees, read some of their writings, and maintained a connection with them for nine years. Given their teaching that procreation was a great evil, and that sexual intercourse was to be avoided, it is strange that his taking of a mistress should have roughly coincided with his joining them.

Manes had been put to death by the Persians in the previous century. It is not possible here to give more than a sketchy notion of his teaching. In the beginning there were two Principles, one Good, one Evil, God and Satan. Each had his own Kingdom, of Light and of Darkness, each organized with a brain-testing complexity. Satan invaded the Kingdom of Light. God took no part in the actual fighting, but emanated Primal-Man (not Adam), who emanated Five Sons. Satan won and devoured all six of them: they remained as Elements of Light in the Kingdom of Darkness. The

Kingdom of Light sent Aeons to help men—one of them Jesus (not Jesus of Nazareth, who was a devil). And so on. Augustine speaks of his "taking food to the Elect that in the factory of their stomachs it should turn into angels and deities by whom I was to be set free." Cicero would have thought it insane. Monica ordered her son out of her house, but seeing in a dream his ultimate conversion, she soon had him back.

Little of all this phantasmagoria appears in the *Confessions*. Two things Augustine got from the Manichees. One was the picture of a God wholly bodily; the other was the assurance that any evil he committed was the work of another will not his, just as the evil in the universe was the work of another Power not God.

Before he joined the Manichees, on through the years when he stayed with them "because he could find nothing better," and after he left them to the very end of his life, these two problems, of the nature of God and the cause of evil, were never out of his mind. "I could not think of God save as a bodily magnitude, because it seemed that what was not such was nothing at all: this indeed was the principal and practically the sole cause of my error" (5.10). "It seemed to me degrading to believe that You had the shape of our human flesh and were circumscribed within the bodily outlines of our limbs." Yet he could see no alternative. The best he could do was think God was a "luminous immeasurable body, and I a particle broken from it."

In all this, he tells us, he got no help at all from the Catholic faith. He simply assumed that the Church taught that as man was in the image of God, God must be like man, body and all. Indeed he seems to have had no instruction worth mentioning in the years of his boyhood. Ever since I first read the phrase of Jean-Paul

Richter—"If we don't use our eyes to see with, we shall use them to weep with"—I have been haunted by it. I cannot escape the feeling that if Monica had wept less and read more, Augustine would not have had to wait for the sermons of Ambrose to inform him of some pretty elementary doctrines. But could she read, I wonder?

It is hard to be sure. She would be startled when her son called on her to take part in the dialogues at Cassiciacum before his baptism—surely such lofty matters were for men. Augustine's answer was twofold: (1) she had made such progress in wisdom that she feared neither suffering nor death—in this he could only be her disciple (nonsense, she said); (2) she knew some of the great books (but he adds that she had heard him reading them aloud); and we find him telling her that philosophy is a Greek word meaning wisdom.

At twenty-eight he had left Carthage for Rome, tricking Monica in order to get away without her. He found teaching Rhetoric in Rome more agreeable than in Carthage, the students were better behaved, but they had the habit of vanishing when the time came for paying their fees. He applied for and got a Professorship of Rhetoric in Milan. Because the Emperors' main concern was guarding the frontier against the barbarians, they had moved out of Rome, and Milan had become a kind of capital city. There the bishop was Ambrose.

And there Monica joined Augustine and his mistress. They must have made an odd trio. Was it there, I wonder, that Augustine first said "Whether it's a wife or a mother, it is still Eve that we must beware of in any woman?" Certainly he does speak of "the heritage of Eve" in Monica. An incident during the country vacation at Cassiciacum suggests that she could have had her trying moments.

She heard a young man singing the verse of a psalm "joyously and noisily" in the lavatory. "She abused him roundly" *(objurgavit eum)*. He laughed her off—"If I were locked in there, must God not be allowed to hear my voice?" Augustine of course talked sensibly to him. *(De ordine* I.8). This incident apart, Monica shows very pleasantly in that period between his conversion and his baptism. Clearly the thirty year strain was over.

Ambrose was one of the greatest of bishops. He had established the relation between the spiritual and temporal orders when he had risked instant death by refusing to let the Emperor Theodosius enter the Cathedral in Milan till he had done public penance for a massacre. Augustine does not mention this in the *Confessions,* but he was impressed by the chant which Ambrose had introduced into the West from the Eastern Church.

Augustine did not manage to get any personal discussion of his problems with Ambrose—though the Bishop's door was always open and Augustine could come in. But even a bishop less busy than Ambrose might have shrunk from discussion with Augustine: he may not have realized the vastly superior power of Augustine's mind, but a Professor of Rhetoric "eager for argument" would need more time than Ambrose had to spare. In every time and place there tends to be a professor who might join the Church (most of them don't): it is barely possible that the Roman patrician may have found Augustine's African accent just too lacerating.

At least Augustine learnt from Ambrose's sermons that the Catholic faith was not what he had thought it was; his figurative interpretations of Scripture answered a lot of Augustine's objections. He was still not sure that the Catholic faith was true, but it might be. Anyhow he was even more uncertain of Manicheeism. He became a Catechumen—on the fringe of the Church, not yet baptized, hoping to move in some day. "I wanted to be as certain of things unseen as that seven and three make ten. And as usually happens, the man who has tried a bad doctor is afraid to trust even a good one."

"If only I had been able to conceive of a substance that was spiritual. . . ."

With this we reach the end of Book 6, with Augustine's mistress sent away, a new mistress taken.

> When first I knew You, You lifted me up so that I might see that there was something to see, but that I was not yet the man to see it. You beat back the weakness of my gaze, blazing upon me too powerfully, and I was shaken with love and dread. . . . I heard Your voice as if from on high: "I am the food of grown men. Grow and you shall eat me." I entered into my own depths with You as my guide.

One might dwell on that "I saw that there was something to see but that I was not yet the man to see it." It marks the turning point —and for many besides Augustine. He at least had come to see God as incorruptible and inviolable and unchanging. "My heart cried out passionately against all my picturings and I tried with this one truth to beat away all that circling host of unrealities from the sight of my mind. But they were scarce gone for the space of a single glance."

The growing took four more torturing years. He could not see how an infinite, immeasurable God *could* have parts—elements in Him that were not the whole of Him. Yet how could He be everywhere, or indeed anywhere, unless He *had* parts? He tried to think up images which would leave God material yet believable—God as light which penetrates the air, filling every part of it; or God as an infinite ocean with creation a sponge filled in every crevice by it. Yet whatever image he could think up always meant "that a larger part of creation would have more of You—the body of an elephant would have more of You than the body of a sparrow." And that was an idea his mind could not live comfortably with.

At this point comes a prayer which is the very essence of Augustine:

> Where in silence I sought so vehemently, the voiceless contritions of my soul were strong cries to Your mercy.

The "mercy" meant that he read some books of the Platonists —neo-Platonists actually, Plato was over seven hundred years dead! There had been a splendid Plato revival led by Plotinus who had been teaching in Rome over a century before Augustine. Marius Victorinus had translated him and other neo-Platonists into Latin: this may indeed have been a special point of God's mercy, for Augustine's Greek was hardly up to that level.

Aided by Plotinus he at last saw the meaning of spirit. Augustine was an artist, with the imagination of an artist. Now he realized that the difficulties about God were all in the imagination, which makes mental pictures, not in the intellect. Without space and time imagination cannot function. Plotinus showed Augustine that neither is essential to existence, that God is wholly beyond them. Space, putting it crudely, is emptiness, and why should emptiness be essential to existence? If a being has parts, of course, it needs space to spread its parts in. But parts are dividedness, and why should dividedness be essential to existence? Why should there not be spiritual beings wholly contained in their being and their action, in the one single act of being?

[26]

It may be that Plotinus helped Augustine even more to see his own soul as in its proper being beyond space and time, yet in its union with a body conditioned by both. He showed him, what he was already feeling towards, that all the excellences of the material world owed such being as they had to such reflection as they were capable of making of their "originals" in the mind of the Absolute. And in his thinking on all this, Augustine came to see that evil has no being of its own, so that the problem of who created it does not arise. It is only the absence, through men's misuse of their wills, of good which ought to be present.

Humanly speaking, Plotinus was essential at this stage of Augustine's growth, quieting his mind and heart about his two torturing problems. But the God of Plotinus was too impersonal, too remote from the vivid dialogue Augustine had so long been having with God. Plotinus could not have used phrases like "God of my heart," "most sweet God."

In fact Plotinus would not have used the word God for his Absolute—his words are the ONE, the GOOD. Nor was it the God of Scripture. He insists that nothing whatever can be said about the ONE, words are only signals to indicate a direction for the soul. It can move toward, aspire toward, the ONE, but the ONE cannot move toward, aspire toward, the soul. "When the soul prays, there is no question of a will that grants the petition. Some influence may fall from the being he is addressing, but that being itself perceives nothing of it." One cannot help thinking of the sun, so life-giving, so unaware.

It is no surprise to learn that Plotinus had spent some time in the Punjab. Neo-Platonism was a compound of Plato, Hinduism and the genius of Plotinus. His absolute was totally impersonal; and the

vivid, sometimes flaming, personality of Augustine could not see any genuine contact with a being which was beyond caring or even knowing. He had been too long in conversation with God.

As Augustine notes, the neo-Platonists of his time were actually using the phrase, "In the beginning was the Word." But of "the Word made flesh" they could make no meaning, nor in the Word suffering and redeeming could they see any point. It is too great a simplification to say that Redemption for the neo-Platonists was simply a process of self-discovery leading the mind to the realm of Ideas, and so to the mystical contemplation of the One. There was more to Plotinus than that, but that was basic.

And it was surely part of the divine mercy that Augustine's attachment to Christ and need for Christ were growing vast. Plotinus forced him to read the Epistles: as he read them, he was first happy to feel that Paul was a Platonist, in the end happiest of all to find that he was not.

III

The struggle for a believable God was close to its end. He was growing in the awareness and the love of Christ, though, as he tells us, there was much about him that he did not yet see aright. He had lost all his desire for worldly success. But he still felt that life would be impossible without a woman. "My two wills, one old, one new, one carnal, one spiritual, were in conflict, and in their conflict wasted my soul."

As against the certainty of God's truth "there was simply nothing I could answer save only laggard laziness; 'Soon,' 'Quite soon,' 'Give me just a little while.' But 'soon' and 'quite soon' did not mean any particular time; and 'just a little while' went on for quite a long while.'' Anyone who has ever had to struggle against this or indeed any temptation—i.e., fight for virtue against himself, ''a controversy about myself against myself''—will meet himself in Book Eight.

The end came suddenly but spectacularly. An African in a high position in the Imperial Court told him and his closest friend Alypius about St. Antony and the hermits of the Egyptian desert, and about two men, officials like himself, who ''having read the life of Antony, had given up everything to embrace the same austere life.'' Hearing of them, Augustine says, ''God set me before my own face that I might see how vile I was, how twisted and unclean and spotted and ulcerous. . . . There I was, going mad on my way to sanity, dying on my way to life, aware how evil I was, unaware that I was to grow better in a little while.''

Torn every way within himself, raging against himself, he went out into the garden. There came that last struggle of lust which we have already met, ''Those trifles of all trifles, those vanities of vanities, my one time mistresses, held me back, plucking at my garment of flesh and murmuring softly, 'Are you sending us away?' . . . 'From this moment shall this and that not be allowed you?' ''

There came a storm of tears. Then he heard a child's voice repeating again and again—in some game, perhaps, though Augustine could not remember such a game—''Take and read, take and read.'' He opened the copy of St. Paul that Alypius had with him and found himself reading, ''Not in rioting and drunkenness, not in lechery and impurities, not in contention and envy, but put ye on the Lord Jesus Christ and make not provision for the flesh and its concupiscences'' (Romans 13:13).

[34]

In the moment his indecision vanished. "How lovely I suddenly found it to be free from the unloveliness of those vanities, so that now it was a joy to renounce what I had been afraid to lose. . . . Now my mind was free from the cares that had gnawed it, from aspiring and getting and weltering in filth and rubbing the scab of lust. And I talked with You as friends talk."

He gave up his Chair of Rhetoric. He had the brief country vacation we have already mentioned at Cassiciacum with a group of friends and was to publish some of the conversations—edited for publication, obviously—which he and they had had there. One of them, *De Magistro,* is between himself and his son, the sixteen-year-old Adeodatus, who was to die soon after—"His great intelligence filled me with a kind of awe." Considering the vastness of his own intelligence, it is pleasant to think of his being awestruck at his son's. Fathers seldom feel like this. But Augustine really did. Later he would quote Cicero's statement that his son was the only man by whom he should rejoice in being surpassed.

Augustine and Monica planned to return to Africa. They got as far as the port of Ostia, where they had the marvellous conversation in which they mounted together through the levels of being. "And while we were talking of His Wisdom and panting for it, with all the effort of our hearts we did in one instant attain to touch it."

Within a week Monica was dead. His iron effort to control his grief ended and he let his tears flow: "making of my tears a pillow for my heart."

Here in Book 9 of the *Confessions* the narrative ends. There is still to come the wonderful examination of his conscience in Book 10, and the three Books on the first chapter of Genesis. One is at first puzzled to find these. I remember wondering if perhaps a secretary gathered them up with the other ten and took them to be copied, and Augustine let them stand. But at every reading I see that the *Confessions* would be as incomplete without them as Genesis would be without its own first chapter.

IV

With Alypius Augustine returned to Tagaste, both of them determined to live in the same house—an embryo monastery in which others began to join them. They did not see themselves as monks but as laymen committed to life with God, in close contact with the daily life of the Church. As such they had to face one peril of which the modern Catholic knows nothing—the peril of being forced, almost kidnapped, into becoming bishops. Tagaste did in fact get Alypius. Augustine avoided visiting any place in which there was a vacancy. His caution did not save him. He went to Hippo, which had a bishop, Valerian. At Mass the Bishop spoke so pointedly, that the congregation gave Augustine no choice. They would not let him leave the church till he had promised—that being the established method!

He was ordained priest in due course and soon after was made an auxiliary bishop—that was a rarity. What may have caused more surprise was that, in a day when it was normal for only bishops to preach, Valerian had him preaching at once—and within two years to bishops, at a Council of the whole African hierarchy!

Augustine established his "monastery" in Hippo—very vegetarian, no women allowed inside, the monks giving what money they had to charity. He trained them well—ten or eleven of them became bishops. And he saw being a bishop as his own function. Preaching

at the consecration of a bishop he said, "Being a bishop doesn't consist in sitting in the episcopal chair—any more than a scarecrow in a vineyard is a watchman."

Even to think of how Augustine spent his days is fatiguing. He was at everyone's disposal—Catholics, heretics, pagans. They thronged his office, sought his advice on family matters; he visited such of his flock as happened to be in jail, used his influence to stop torture and execution, visited the sick. They brought him their legal difficulties and accepted his judgments. All these things, in his own mind, were peripheral, souls were what he was a bishop about! He preached most days, answered letters from all over the Roman world. A hundred sermons and well over two hundred letters have come down to us. As Peter Brown reminds us, in St. *Augustine of Hippo,* though he never went back to Italy and no one in the Papal Court or the Emperor's Court had seen him, the fame of his mind spread everywhere.

But everywhere was not his concern, Hippo was, and Africa came to be. In its three hundred dioceses there was a Catholic bishop and a Donatist bishop. The Donatists were the result of a schism going back into the third century and turned into a sect forty years before Augustine was born. They demanded moral purity for all Christians, would not re-admit to full membership those who had once failed. Bishops who had yielded to persecution even for a time could never again be accepted as bishops. Probably a majority of the Christians of Africa were Donatists. Augustine preached against them, wrote against them, and debated with them. Father van der Meer gives a detailed account in *Augustine the Bishop.* He wrote a hymn against them, twenty stanzas each beginning with the different letters of the alphabet, in order. Meanwhile he was waging a one-man war against his one-time associates, the Manichees.

None of this appears in the *Confessions,* which he wrote a few years after Valerian's death had made the see of Hippo his. He does not even mention that he was a bishop. There is not a hint of the turmoil round him as he wrote; the book might have been written in an ivory tower. There is almost nothing in it to date it. Girls to whom I dictated my translation thought I was telling my own story, so wholly modern it reads! It is of every date. It names a single Emperor, Valentinian (without saying which one), it names no popes. Augustine's brother Navigius appears once, he doesn't mention his sister. The names he gives are of people who affected the issue of the struggle of this one sinner to win God's mercy.

Half way through his episcopate the most mentally exacting struggle of all began. Pelagius—Roman Britain's solitary great heretic—saw salvation as within the compass of man's natural powers, the supernatural life of grace not needed. Augustine saw this as a kind of root and branch denial of the very meaning of Christ. He threw himself totally into the controversy. His health was already badly broken, *and* he was writing *The City of God,* which might well have been any other man's lifework. There had been a revival of intellectual Paganism, linked with the idea that the sack of Rome by Alaric in 410 was the result of abandoning the old traditions which had served Rome for a thousand years in favor of a lot of nonsense about a Jew the Romans had very sensibly crucified; there were plenty who thought the disaster was the vengeance of the old gods for Rome's apostasy. Augustine wrote his book in answer. He gave seventeen years to it.

As nobody now believes in the old gods, the book might strike us as a sheer waste of seventeen years. As Christopher Dawson says, Augustine's worrying about Donatists and Pelagians and pagan gods while civilisation was on the verge of the Dark Ages, "would seem like the activity of an ant which works on while its nest is being destroyed." And indeed when he died in 430 the Vandals were besieging his city. "But," Dawson goes on, "to Augustine the ruin of civilization and the destruction of the Empire were not very important things. He looked beyond the aimless and bloody chaos of history to the world of eternal realities." What matters in the *City of God* is its explanation of its own title: "Two loves built two cities, the love of self to the contempt of God built the City of the World [which he calls Babylon], the love of God to the contempt of self the City of God [which he calls Jerusalem]. By what a man loves he can tell to which city he belongs."

Notice that this vast book was his response to a situation. Except for the *Confessions* and the *Trinity,* every book he wrote was in some sort occasional, written to meet a challenge. Writing against the Manichees, he had to emphasize the power of the human will; against the Pelagians, he had to stress its inadequacy without grace. Pelagius could quote an early work of Augustine in support of his own case against Augustine. There was no time to attend to that sort of balancing. He thought aloud, so to speak, on Predestination, returning to it again and again: Lutherans and Calvinists can quote him against Catholics, and Catholics quote him back at them. He produced no over-all system, nor, apart from the *Trinity,* any systematic treatment of any one doctrine.

The reason should be obvious. He was so immeasurably busy as a bishop with what had to be done there and then, all day and every day, that it is a marvel that he wrote at all. One is tempted to think that a wise Church would have relieved him of all extra labors, leaving him to pray, study, write. But then again all that poured into his writing from continuing contact with humanity as it is would not have poured. He did not simply observe the human struggle, as every theologian should and many do; he was right down where it was happening, involved in it, affecting its issue.

Reading over this Introduction I feel its sketchiness. All the great matters—Manicheeism, Neo-Platonism, Donatism, Pelagianism—deserve better. I have tried to say only enough about each topic to make the Prayers comprehensible. It is too much to hope I have not denatured any of them in the process.

THE GREAT BUSINESS OF PRAYING

PRAYING FOR WHAT HE WANTED

Grant me, O Lord, to know which is the soul's first movement towards You—to implore Your aid or to utter its praise of You (1.1).

In the order of time, our first movement towards God—as towards everyone else indeed—is to implore, for we are aware of our wants before we are aware even of our existence.

Prayer is conversation with God, our Father, telling Him in all naturalness everything that concerns us. And our wants concern us deeply. But no conversation with anyone can consist wholly of asking for things, and in our conversation with God we should progress from thinking about ourself to thinking about Him, from talking about ourself to talking about Him. Our prayer should move from telling Him of our wants, to thanking Him for His gifts, on through sorrow for what has gone wrong in our relation with Him, to adoration and love. At every level sincerity is of the essence. And

[43]

we are intensely sincere in asking for what we want. One is far advanced in holiness whose adoration has the intense sincerity of his asking!

To return to Augustine's question, we note that the first prayer he reports is quite specially an imploring:

> Praying to You, small as I was but with no small energy, that I might not be flogged at school (1.9).

We need no assurance of the sincerity of that. After sixteen centuries we can still hear the wail in it and the indignation of the small boy at parents (yes, Monica too) who laughed over the floggings he got. But the sincerity was all concentrated on what he wanted—*his* will, not God's. And as he tells us it was rooted in insincerity—he was simply not doing the studies whose non-doing brought the floggings. Why not? Because he loved games—at which he admits that he cheated extravagantly.

Of this sort of asking-prayer Augustine does not give many examples. The most notable comes after his conversion but before his baptism. At a time when he and his friends were together in the country house at Cassiciacum and he did some writing—"now in God's service but still smacking of the school of pride"—he remembers what inner goads God used in order to tame him.

But there was one outer goad too:

> I have not forgotten the bite of Your scourge. You sent me the torture of toothache. . . . As soon as we had gone on our knees in all simplicity, the pain went.

I think there is a real problem for us here. The believer has a tendency to think that all his sufferings, in faith or morals or finance,

in mind or body or relations with others, are sent to him individually by God. "Why does God do this to me?" He may say it resentfully, as one who has deserved better of God—like Léon Bloy saying to God: "I would not treat a mongrel dog as You treat me." He may accept in all humility—God must have thought he needed that particular trial.

In a given case it might be so, but the humility and the resentment alike may miss the point. We live in a universe of laws—physical and mental and moral laws. If we collide with one of them, suffering follows. Certain causes produce certain effects—pleasant effects, painful effects; otherwise we could not grow in our knowledge of the world, still less in the mastery of it which God meant for us.

When suffering comes, therefore, our normal reaction should be to ask what law has been broken, by ourselves or others. God does not guarantee that in all circumstances I can avoid suffering provided I pray—that a tidal wave may drown, an earthquake may swallow, or a famine starve, everyone but me. He does guarantee that suffering which is not caused by our own fault can be turned by Him to our advantage; so can even the suffering we *have* deserved if we turn to Him. There seems to be no doubt, for instance, that the Jews emerged cleansed and strengthened from their forty years' captivity in Babylon.

Though we need not assume a special divine "sending" for every pain of mind or body, yet God *can* send suffering. The Epistle to the Hebrews comments on the phrase from Proverbs—"The Lord disciplines him whom He loves." And Augustine cries out: *"You are breaking my bones asunder with the rod of Your discipline."*

That sort of discipline indeed could be part of God's training of those whom he has chosen for some great work: Augustine had a mighty work to do for God; he needed more disciplining than most; he knew it, and it looks as if he got it.

Augustine is not against our asking God for what in the natural way of wanting we want. And though I am not sure he saw how abnormal it would be if we did *not* ask our Father for whatever we feel would make us happy, he certainly saw no evil in our asking for anything not sinful—health, success in studies or business (be careful), a wife (be very careful). But our relation to God is what life is about. "Those who find their joy in things external easily fall into emptiness and in their starved minds lick shadows."

The danger of emptiness, futility, is a continuing thread in his thinking. "They have received their reward, empty men, empty reward." Like other Catholics I ask saints to join their prayers to mine for things I want. It would not occur to me to ask Augustine— I feel he would almost certainly think I'd be less empty without them. This is nonsense, of course. But sensation *is* sensation.

His steady warning is that we are bad judges of what will make us happy: and indeed most of us will find our past littered with things we longed for and either got and wished we hadn't, or did not get and lived to be glad we hadn't. Happiness, as Augustine sees it, is always the by-product of a right relation to reality. "Today my pity is more for the sinner getting enjoyment from his sins than when he suffers torment from the loss of pleasure which is ultimately destructive, happiness which is only penuriousness."

In a comment on Psalm 91:8 he puts this more pungently; of the evil-doer who appears to be happy he writes: "He is not happy, he is like a sick man laughing in his delirium."

Augustine summarizes his views on what we should ask God for in his Letter to Proba. Fultonia Proba—a rich woman of the powerful family of the Anicii—had come to Carthage after Alaric's sack of Rome; she had written to ask what he thought of Paul's "We know not what we should pray for" (Romans 8:26). To be happy, wrote Augustine. And what is happiness? He quotes Psalm 27: "One thing have I asked of the Lord, this will I seek after, that I may dwell in the house of the Lord all the days of my life."

By living in "the house of the Lord" the Psalmist, I suppose, meant being constantly in the Temple. Augustine sees it as living in closeness to God, loving Him, adoring Him, harmonizing our will with His will—praying (for ourselves and others) for eternal salvation hereafter, and on this earth for a clear vision of ourselves, for God's aid against temptation, for His mercy when we have sinned.

We shall look at Augustine's own praying in the reverse order, as it concerned Sin, Self-knowledge, Adoration, and Love.

It may seem strange that thanksgiving is not in the list. But there is not much explicit thanking in the *Confessions*. There is none at all in the Our Father, which for Augustine was the ideal prayer: but the whole of it is a cry of gratitude, and so is the whole of the *Confessions*. I think where we say "thank" he tends to say "praise"—as in *"Praise to you, glory to you, Fountain of mercies, I became more wretched and you closer to me."*

I need hardly say that he did not break up his praying into categories like this. I fear that I may seem to be reducing Augustine's forest to a formal garden; but I do not see how we are to learn from his prayers otherwise. Do, please, read the *Confessions*. In his own praying he often gives the impression that sin, self, salvation, adoration and love were all trying to get themselves uttered at once.

[50]

The great business of praying is broken off through the onrush of every idle thought.

If even Augustine suffered from distractions in prayer, we ourselves had better be careful. He warns us "Don't let the ears of your heart be deafened by the clamors of your folly."

PRAYING AGAINST HIS SINS

Augustine loved the Lord's Prayer. Half of it is concerned with our sinfulness. So is half of all his own praying. Newman could speak of "two luminous certainties," God and himself. Augustine had the same two certainties, perhaps even more luminously. As we have noted, he did not mean, any more than Newman was to mean, that nothing else existed for him, only that nothing else was so continuously present to him, of nothing else was he so at-every-moment aware. And what he was most aware of in himself was his worthlessness. "I find myself hateful."

I

"In my youth I became to myself a wasteland." Even after his conversion he could say "The house of my soul is narrow, ruinous, littered with filth." He prayed desperately to God to enlarge it, rebuild it, clean it.

> From my secret sins cleanse me, O Lord, and from those of others spare Your servant. O Christ for Your sacred Name's sake, for Your bitter Passion's sake, for Your infinite Mercy's sake, forgive and forget what I have been, pity O pity what I am, satisfy for what I deserve and grant what I desire.

This was his state by the time he came to write the *Confessions*, fifteen years or so after his entry into the Church, five or six years after he had been consecrated bishop. At the moment of his conversion he could not have written it (any more than he could have moved so easily from asking God to asking Christ). He had not yet realized that chastity was altogether beyond his, or any man's, natural powers. He had read "I can do all things in Christ who strengthens me" (Philippians 4:13). But his mind had not lingered on it. He still felt that he must win the fight himself *before* becoming a Christian. He had not yet seen that he must simply throw himself in naked trust upon the strength of God.

In the ferocity of the struggle which ended in his seeing it, the Augustine was formed who saw how deadly an enemy was Pelagius, with his belief in human nature's sufficiency for salvation. Both of them could say that to be virtuous one had only to will it. But Pelagius said it light-heartedly: since it was true, man did not need supernatural grace. Augustine said it in the irony of anguish—in full realization of the powerlessness of the unaided will.

He learnt it in a new dimension from his experience as priest and bishop, coping with the chaos of wills in the flock entrusted to him: monks, priests, laity. In the coping he had the new anguish of the certainty that he would be called in judgment for any of them who might be lost eternally. He certainly grew more pessimistic about human weakness and wickedness as the years passed, "the bitter sea of the human race"; and his flock got the sour taste of themselves in his sermons. He describes, for instance, the mourners at a funeral, all serious and solemn: "from the graveyard they return to their swindling, stealing, lying, to their drunkenness and all the body's lusts. . . . The fact that they have just buried a man becomes

a reason for living sensibly—let us eat and drink for tomorrow we'll die too.''

The upshot is that optimism about salvation is madness, and dangerous madness. Yet despair is one of the most grievous and needless of sins.

> You can cleanse us from our habit and You are merciful to the sins of those who confess to You. And You hear the groans of those still chained in their sin, and You loose us from the chains we have made for ourselves.

> But we can refuse:

> All this You do unless we raise against You the arrogance of a sham liberty.

To use the phrase which has become a cliché: we must pray as though everything depended on God (which it does), we must act as though everything depended on us (which also, in its own different way, it does). We cannot save ourselves without God. But God cannot save us without us, so to speak, against the thrust of our will: to compel our will would be to treat us as non-men. Only God can give us the light and the strength without which we cannot be saved. But we must use them. He has no will to damn us, only our refusal can do that.

II

O Lord my God, how deep is the abyss of Your secret, and how far from it have the consequences of my sins held me. (10.3)

[54]

Like all sinners Augustine was fascinated by the sins to which he was specially tempted. But few of us are as fascinated as he by the psychological problem of sin. Given that we know better, why do we do worse?

We know that we are in a universe made by God of nothing, that we are held in existence therefore by no element in ourselves, but solely by God's will to sustain us in being. It sounds like sheer imbecility to think we can gain happiness against the will without which we should fall back into the original nothingness from which that will drew us.

A man I knew kept at me for forty years with the taunt "If I believed what Catholics say they believe, I wouldn't sin, I wouldn't dare to and I wouldn't want to." I never satisfied him. I wonder if Augustine could have. For this problem bothered him to the end, as a problem not about mankind but about himself. Early it brought him close to madness. Sanity lay in discovering why he could not wholly answer it. He came to see enough of the mystery of God and the lesser mystery of himself to be able to live with the problem, and so with God, and so with himself.

It is in one's own most observable sin that the problem is best studied. His was sexual. But his fullest analysis of a sin concerns one with nothing of sex in it.

He had gone with a group of boys to steal all the pears off a neighbor's tree. I have kept no count of the number of times I have read that Augustine made a ridiculous fuss about having stolen some pears. Clearly the writers had not read the *Confessions* recently. What concerned him was *why* he had done it. "We carried off an immense load of pears, not to eat—for we barely tasted them before throwing them to the hogs.'' The only pleasure in the act was that it was forbidden. ''I loved the evil in me, not the thing for which I did the evil, simply the evil.''

There follows (2.6) a listing of all the excellences in God of which our different sins are a parody, this being a key to his thinking on sin: of what excellence in God was this idiotic pear-stealing a parody? Perhaps he got ''a deceptive sense of omnipotence from doing something forbidden without immediate punishment.'' He ponders over possible explanations and concludes:

> Who can unravel that complex twisted knottedness. . . . In my youth I strayed too far from Your sustaining power, and I became to myself a waste land.

The problem never left him, but he got occasional gleams of light. He wrote to Proba in the letter I have quoted: ''The soul, housed in a corruptible body, is affected by a kind of earthy contagion.'' But it is of prime importance that he came to see (as against the Platonists) that the worst sins were neither in the body nor caused by it. Pride, arrogance, envy were far worse. Not in liberation from the body lay the spirit's perfection. ''The mind has more control of its body than of itself!''

So the problem is how to account for sin in the soul. To the end, Augustine could not be clear, and would not pretend to be clear, whether each soul was created direct by God (which made the problem darker) or, in some way he could not conceive, issued from the parents (which only pushed the darkness a step back). At any rate the sin was in the will. Yet how could it be? For just as the eye is made for the seeing of color and what is not colored cannot be seen by it, so the will is made to desire what is good and what is not good cannot be desired by it. But how can a faculty sin, if it is incapable of desiring what is not good?

His answer to that question could fill a book. But the key to it is in one phrase: "by loving the part as though it were the whole." The whole is good and can be desired; the parts are good too, and they too can be desired. But if in desiring individual things or people we leave out—worse, if we deliberately cast out—the whole of which they are parts, we sin. We can love creatures instead of God, to the rejection of God. We can love sexuality, our own or another's, as if it were the whole of the personality. Augustine speaks of the madness, which had been so strong in him but is not special to him, of "not knowing how to love men as men"—that is, as they are, in themselves and in their relation to God.

Since we can desire anything that seems good to us, we can desire incompatibles. We can really desire what God wills for us, but we can really desire what God has forbidden—"My two wills, one old one new, one carnal one spiritual, were in conflict, and in their conflict laid my soul waste."

> O loveliness that does not deceive. I collect myself out of that broken state in which my being was torn asunder because I was turned away from You, the One, and wasted upon the many.

III

It was what Augustine learnt by his fight for sexual control that gave him the key to such understanding of sin in general as he managed to attain. He has savage things to say against lust of the flesh: in the sex-sinner, for instance, he finds a double resemblance to Lazarus—he is not only dead, he stinks. Yet he does not see sexual sin as the worst of sins—pride, arrogance, envy, hate, treachery, cruelty, to name a few, are far worse. But it was the most clinging, the hardest to be rid of; it was the most obsessive, claiming the whole of a man's attention; and it was quasi-universal, just about everyone feels the pull of it; he himself still felt it. He shocked some of his fellow bishops by suggesting that St. Paul might have felt it. If only Augustine had been freed from the slavery of his office for the time it would have taken him to write the commentary he had planned on Paul's Epistles!

Grant me chastity, but not yet.

In all the centuries since, there is no sinner who has not heard his own voice in that cry. Whatever our special temptations, we have much to learn about ourselves from Augustine's acute, unsparing analysis of his.

There was his feeling that life without sex intercourse would be altogether unbearable. As his vision of God grew truer and clearer he was torn two ways agonizingly—"going mad on my way to sanity."

I was ravished to You by Your beauty, yet soon was torn from You again by my own weight. . . . Carnal habit was that weight (1.17).

One of his greatest phrases is "Amor meus pondus meum": "My love is my weight; wherever I go, it is my love that takes me there." Bodies rise or fall according to what they weigh. In souls the decisive factor is what they love—according to that, they rise or they fall. And carnal love still held him.

(Thus) in the thrust of a trembling glance my mind had arrived at that which is . . . but I lacked the strength to hold my gaze fixed . . . so that I returned to my old habits, bearing nothing with me but a memory of delight and a desire for something of which I had caught the fragrance but which I had not yet the strength to eat (7.17).

In the Eighth Book he examines his "chastity, but not yet"— he had been afraid that God would hear his prayer too soon, with lust still offering delights beyond his refusing.

My soul tossed and turned, on back and sides and belly, and the bed was always hard: for You alone are our rest (6.16).

This last he had said after his mistress had been sent away. But even after the story of St. Antony in the Egyptian desert had forced him to see himself as "vile and twisted and ulcerous" so that at last he "stood naked in his own sight," lust would not let him go. Sex straight, so to speak, and sex obscene "plucked at the garment of my flesh. . . . And then I began to hear them not half so loud, they were softly muttering behind my back."

Yet he could not wrench himself free. Read the rest of the scene in the garden at Milan—the child's voice calling "Take and read," Augustine opening the Bible at Romans 13:13—"not in lechery and licentiousness. . . ."

Observe that he does not blame God when his prayers for aid against sexual sin, or any sin, seem to leave him still in sin's grip. Adam could blame "the woman You gave me"—he hadn't asked for a wife, God had wished Eve on him, now look what she had done to him. In our own day we have progressed a step: we blame God for

the self he gave us—we hadn't asked to be born, God had willed into existence the self we are, really it is his problem.

Augustine will have none of this. He knows whose fault it is. When he says, "Remember that we are dust and it was You who made us so," he says it not as blaming God, but as a plea for God's mercy. Nor does he ever doubt that all his womanizing is sinful. He shows no sign of feeling that it is maturing or enriching. He makes no excuse for it at all. What he is saying boils down to "I like sex and that's about the size of it."

Cicero's *Hortensius,* which had started him on the upward road, agrees with Plato that genital activity gets in the way of the mind's. But Augustine felt much more than that. Christ (Mark 7) had listed not only adultery but fornication among the sins that defile a man, make him unclean. And Augustine, even before his conversion, felt it so.

One notes only that we do not find in the *Confessions* what strikes us as a depth of promiscuity's uncleanness—namely that it involves not only the reduction of the self to a physical craving but the reduction of the other party to a convenience for the craving's relief. Augustine makes no reference to what his "vileness" may have meant to the women. There is not a hint of what her fifteen years with him may have meant to his mistress. And not a word about the twelve-year-old and what she might have felt about being jilted by him.

The first girl he had fallen in love with at Carthage—because he was "in love with love"—flits in for a single sentence, then vanishes forever. Some of the ladies of his youth must have looked in to hear him preach; their memories would have made concentration on the sermon difficult for them—for him too if he saw them.

We may be puzzled at his failure to advert to what his sex conduct may have meant to his partners in it. Certainly it arose from no refusal to face the facts about himself, nor from any unwillingness to show to others his conduct at its worst.

> Being not yet filled with You, I am a burden to myself. The pleasures of this life for which I should weep are in conflict with the sorrows of this life in which I should rejoice, and I know not on which side is the victory. Woe is me, Lord, have pity on me.

Remember it is a bishop who is writing, a bishop wanting light about himself.

PRAYING FOR SELF-KNOWLEDGE

You were there before me, but I had gone away from myself, and I could not find even myself, much less You.

The key word in our world this last year and for a few years before that was identity. Everyone was in search of his identity— who he was, what he was, what was the point of him. Augustine saw that if there is no God, we have no identity: we exist briefly in a universe which is meaningless, since there is no one to mean it, before sinking back into the meaninglessness which wraps us as it wraps all things.

But for those who have found God and given their mind to knowing Him, there is still the need to know themselves. "That darkness," cries Augustine, "is lamentable in which the possibilities in me are hidden from myself. Yet what could be closer to me

than myself?'' Close indeed. Too close to see, perhaps. Only God sees us wholly as we are, sees in us not our self-image but His own image and what we have made of it.

From my secret sins cleanse me, O Lord.

By ''secret sins'' Augustine means sins that God sees and we do not. There are two levels of these—according as our blindness is real or willed. His sermons are rich in observation of both kinds.

''He who hates is a murderer. No. You have not mixed poisons, not drawn the sword, not hired killers. You have not actually committed a crime. You have simply died inside yourself.'' (Sermon 49).

That is his ''translation'' of Christ's statement that the man who lusts for a woman has committed adultery in his heart. From a different angle of blindness: ''Habit makes every sin come more easily, till at last a man no longer thinks of it as sinful. The organ feels no pain, not because it is healthy but because it is dead.'' (Sermon 172).

Less excusable is willed blindness, fooling oneself. The people he preached to had a habit of showing their feelings—wailing, weeping, beating their breasts as some phrase of his bit home. But he warns them about ''beating our breast as a way of putting a plaster on our sins'': we may be doing it to impress others, but the hypocrite can fool himself too.

Lord, show me to myself, that I may confess to my brethren.

Most sermons on sexual sins leave the sexual sinners in the congregation unmoved—''It's all very well for him. He hasn't my temptations.'' No one ever said this about Augustine's preaching or writing on this or any other sin. He never speaks of sin as a strange habit of other people. Father Damian let his congregation know that he had contracted leprosy by saying "We lepers." In every sermon Augustine seems to be saying "We sinners." He never sees a sin without feeling that he might have committed it himself. He always seems to be feeling "There but for the grace of God go I."

A few pages back we found Augustine speaking of the pleasures of life which still drew him. Book Ten gives some of them. It is the most astounding examination of conscience ever written by a high ecclesiastic. Newman had read it: could he have written anything of the sort?

He was an Englishman, of course, and Augustine an African. But there were hundreds of African bishops, and Augustine's frankness is matched by none of them. It is so frank, yet so determined not to exaggerate. But remember, again, he is examining his conscience under the gaze of God. As he was to say in his Letter to Proba—"If Christ were standing by your side, what would your sins look like—not to Him, but to yourself?"

We have read the prayer immediately on his conversion: "Now it was a joy to renounce what I had been so afraid to lose. . . . Now my mind was free from the cares that gnawed it, from aspiring and getting and weltering in filth and rubbing the scab of lust."

What had happened to the scab of lust in the years between? He writes, "There still lives in my memory the images of those things . . . which my long habit had fixed there. When I am awake they beset me though with no great power, but in sleep not only seeming pleasant, but even to the point of consent and the likeness of the act itself."

It is an evidence of his calm acceptance of Christ's word "To

God all things are possible'' that he hopes God will cleanse even these dreams of his. One sin he mentions may startle us: ''You have already healed me of my craving for revenge.'' Of that craving the *Confessions* have not given a hint—unless we assume that his early habit of cheating in games and fury at defeat may have meant a vengeful desire to be even with those who beat him.

He finds himself in danger of gluttony: ''Drunkenness is far from me and You will have mercy that it may never come near me—but overeating has sometimes crept up on Your servant.

You will have mercy that it may depart from me.

He must have taken his gluttony very seriously to give it the lengthy treatment he does. Yet he had become a vegetarian, and I find it hard to imagine being gluttonous about vegetables.

The pleasures of the senses—his were very keen—got in the way of his thinking and praying. But there seems to be no doubt of the sin he was at this stage most sure of, ''The report of men's mouths brings a most perilous temptation from the love of praise.''

He was not given to ''the ugly savagery of pride,'' which is a positive choice of self in place of God as the object of our love. I feel quite sure he had no conceit, which is a certainty of our own many excellences: one cannot find a trace of awareness in him of the vast power of his intellect. Compared with pride and conceit, vanity, a desire for admiration, may be hardly a sin at all. There is humility in it as not in the other two. Yet there is a kind of silliness in it, and it can lead to foolish decisions. He finds it in himself from boyhood all the way on.

Augustine is determined not to fool himself about himself. I take one example of his self-examination. I summarize: ''One thinks one is eating for health, when in fact one is indulging one's greed. But what suffices for health is too little for enjoyment. This is not the kind of thing I can resolve to cut off once for all, as with fornication. The reins of the throat are to be held somewhere between too lightly and too tightly.''

Enjoyment is what frightens him, so easily it can run away with him. Yet enjoying God's gifts in all naturalness is surely a way of thanking him for them: He had not filled His world with booby traps. Augustine might have found life easier if he could have had Chesterton's attitude: ''Thank God for wine by moderation in the use of it''—or even the Psalmist's: ''Wine that maketh glad the heart of man.''

In Book 10 Augustine has the same kind of close analyzing, anguished yet accurate, of his other sins—vanity especially. He had this very much in mind when he spoke of ''the furnace of the human tongue.''

> Be You our glory. Let us be loved for Your sake and let Your word be praised in us. For when You are our strength it is strength indeed, when it is our own it is all weakness.

Even if these sins are not ours (even if we feel some of them are not sins at all), yet as we read the *Confessions* we meet ourselves, and we see ourselves better for having those sharp eyes looking at us and through us.

Read Book 10 right through. One may end the reading wondering how Augustine can find himself hateful. We wonder if his remorse is an act. If that sort of thing were the worst we could find in ourselves, we should be delighted. We feel rather as when a violinist friend, after playing as it seems to us brilliantly, talks

despairingly of giving up the violin: we feel how glorious it would be if we could play like that. But he is comparing himself not with us but with Paganini. Augustine is comparing himself not with us but with Christ. Never out of his mind is the contrast between himself and the God in whose image he was made.

> Do you, O Lord my God, hear me and see me and pity me and heal me—You under whose eyes I have become a question to myself.

Most bishops, I imagine, talk like that to God. But it is a help to the rest of us to hear one of them doing it. We might even begin to make his prayer our own. . . .

PRAYING FOR SALVATION

I

There is a real problem for us here. Augustine constantly uses the word predestination; but if our eternal future is already settled by God, why was he praying for salvation? Predestination was a problem for him too, as for all who believe in God's omniscience. If God knows eternally all things whatsoever, then He knew before we were born what sins we were going to commit, whether we are going to repent or not, going to be saved or not. What then are we asking Him for?

Augustine saw, of course, that "before" is the wrong word, so is "knew." God's verb has no past tense. God is, and therefore knows, in eternity; and in the total present of eternity the word "before" has no meaning. The *pre* of predestination carries the same error. The problem lies in the relation between man's action in time—with its fluid now, existing on a knife edge between a past that is no more and a future that is not yet—and God's knowledge in the abiding now of eternity, the nature of which we cannot even conceive.

Augustine knew that all this did not answer the question how our freedom can coexist with God's omniscience, it merely made it impossible to phrase the question properly! The problem continued to nag him. As philosopher and theologian he kept coming at it. But it plays no large part in his praying, which is our concern in this book. With the Lord's Prayer ever before the eyes of his mind, he prayed in the certainty that our prayers make a difference.

I I

Very early in his career of sin, a bishop had told his mother (as a reason why *he* should not reason with her son): "The son of those tears cannot perish." Augustine seems to have thought along the same lines. Soon afterwards he went to Rome. "Rome," he says, "welcomed me with the scourge of bodily illness and I nearly went to hell bearing the weight of deadly sin against You and myself and other men, over and above the bond of original sin." He recovered. And he tells God:

> You could not refuse Your help to the tears with which she begged You for the salvation of my soul.

Soon after his conversion Monica died, asking him "Remember me at the altar of the Lord." She was thinking of the cleansing her soul would need in Purgatory. The Book of Revelation (21-27) had told her that nothing unclean shall enter Heaven. She did not think herself perfect, nor indeed did Augustine. Of her decision not to have him baptized as a boy, he remarks that though she was no longer in the center of Babylon she was still lingering in its outer suburbs. And to the end it did not occur to him that she was fitted to enter the presence of the all-pure God. Did he in fact think that anyone else was? "I dare not say that from the moment of her regeneration in baptism no word issued from her mouth contrary to Your command. . . It would go ill with the most praiseworthy life lived by men, if You were to examine it with Your mercy laid aside . . . ."

> Thus my Glory and my Life, God of my heart, leaving aside for this time her good deeds, I now pray to You for my mother's sins. Grant my prayer through the true Medicine of our wounds, who hung upon the cross and who now, sitting at Your right hand, makes intercession for us. . . . From her heart she forgave those who trespassed against her: do You also forgive such trespasses as she may have been guilty of.

She must be prayed for most especially at Mass: "She desired only to be remembered at Your altar, which she had served without ever missing so much as a day on which she knew the Holy Victim was offered. . . . To this sacrament of our redemption Your hand-maid has bound her soul by the bond of Faith" (9.13).

He concludes with a request that concerns far more people than he could possibly have dreamed:

> O my Lord my God, inspire as many of Your servants as may read this, that they may remember at Your altar Your servant Monica, with Patricius her husband.

By now he saw the Mass as our joining with Christ in his offering, continuous in Heaven, of his redeeming sacrifice. And this sacrifice he saw as the way of our salvation. "Who shall restore to him his innocent blood? Who shall give him the price by which he purchased us so as to take us from him?"

PRAYING WITH CHRIST JESUS

If I had not sought the way to You in Christ our Savior, I would have come not to instruction but to destruction. See, Lord, I cast my care upon You, that I may live.

I

When Augustine opened Scripture at the thirteenth chapter of Romans, the last part of the message which sealed his conversion was "Put on the Lord Jesus Christ, and make no provision for the flesh, to satisfy its cravings."

It looks as if he took the words "Put on the Lord Jesus Christ" rather in his stride, as a sort of liturgical end-phrase. When the last stage of the upward movement was beginning, we find him saying: "At least the faith of Your Christ, our Lord and Savior taught by the Catholic Church, stood firm in my heart, though on many points I was still uncertain and swerving from the norm of the doctrine."

It would be well worth anyone's while to trace his earlier attitudes to Christ.

When he was on the point of breaking with the Manichees, he was for a moment attracted by certain skeptical philosophers: "Yet

I absolutely refused to entrust the care of my sick soul to them, because they were without the saving name of Christ." We are startled to come upon this, since it is hard to find in him any earlier sense of devotion to Christ.

There was a long period when he "thought the Savior was the only begotten son, brought forth for our salvation from the mass of God's most luminous substance." But he could not "think" the Incarnation—"If born of the Virgin Mary, then he was mingled with her flesh, and if thus mingled, then defiled." He could not "see the Word made flesh save as the Word defiled by flesh." That flesh was defilement because of its special origin from Satan the Manichees had taught him: he got no help from the Platonists, who saw the body as a prison house from which liberation is essential.

He did his best to escape from a dilemma he found unbearable. Christ is shown in the Gospels as having a body; it must surely be, as some of the earlier Gnostics had held, a phantom body, in which Christ did not really suffer because it was not real. He tells us how in his effort to conquer sin he at that stage got no help from thinking of Christ himself: "How indeed could my sins be healed by the cross of a phantom which at that time I thought You were?" He sums up this stage in a phrase: "I was not yet lowly enough to hold the lowly Jesus as my God."

To read the *Confessions* and then go back to the *Dialogues,* composed by Augustine at Cassiciacum before his baptism by Ambrose, shows what fifteen years of living the Faith—as layman, priest, bishop—had done to him. The thinness of the *Dialogues,* the aroma they exhale of the schools, seems pallid after we have lived along with the full-bloodedness of the *Confessions.*

Not that he had joined the Church as still a neo-Platonist.

Plotinus had helped him to answer certain intellectual difficulties which had stood between him and Christ, so that he could at last accept the Faith in its fullness, though he had barely begun to glimpse what its fullness contained for his exploring. To think of Augustine as a neo-Platonist is to underrate Plotinus—to reduce him to a handful of ideas and to miss the real splendor of his teaching as a whole. He would certainly have refused to regard the Augustine of Cassiciacum as a disciple.

I I

Yet Augustine was still new in the Faith; and only one who has lived it can have any notion of what living it can do to mind and will and the whole man.

The doctrines especially: accepting them is only a beginning. It may fairly be said that when he was baptized by Ambrose he had an immense devotion to Christ, but had not yet seen deep into his role as Redeemer. I have read somewhere a suggestion that it was his realization of this which caused him to ask Bishop Valerian to give him time off for the study of Scripture. He did not take long, a few weeks maybe. But he was an unbelievably fast reader.

Five years or so afterwards, when he came to write the *Confessions,* he had filled that gap. Do read section 12 of Book Four. Paul himself never saw deeper or said what he saw more richly.

> Our Life came down to this earth and took away our death, slew death with the abundance of His own life. . . . He withdrew from our eyes, that we might return to our own heart and find Him. For He went away and behold He is still here. He came into this world to save sinners. Unto Him my soul confesses, for it has sinned against Him.

That is not exactly in the form of a prayer, yet prayer it is. So is the ending of Book Ten.

> The Mediator between God and men, the man Christ Jesus, appeared between sinful mortals and the immortal Just One: for like men He was mortal, like God He was just . . . turning us from slaves into Your sons, by being Your Son and becoming a slave . . . He has redeemed me with His blood. I meditate on the price of my redemption, I eat it and drink it and give it to others to eat and drink.

There we have the full truth about man—spirit is primary but the body has its own immeasurable sacredness. It was essential to Christ's humanity, therefore to ours. Augustine now knows why Paul could call it the temple of the Holy Spirit. Christ's body had its own essential part to play in his redeeming sacrifice, therefore our body has its part to play if we are to make his salvation ours "in fear and trembling." For soul and body Christ is nourishment indispensable.

> From what deep-sunken hiding place was my free-will summoned forth in the moment in which I bowed my neck to Your light yoke and my shoulders to Your light burden, Christ Jesus, my Helper and my Redeemer?

In sermons and in his Commentary on St. John, Augustine was to go the one step further, not only to our membership of Christ's Mystical Body—which is the meaning of that rebirth in Baptism without which Christ tells us man cannot be saved—but to Christ and His members as one single Christ. Writing on "The sheep hear his voice" (John 10:3), he speaks of Shepherd and flock as *Unus Christus amans seipsum*—One Christ, loving Himself.

THE PRAYER OF ADORATION

You are the life of lives, the life of souls, You are livingness itself, and You will not change, O Light of my soul.

I

A Christian may reach a stage where he is untroubled by doubt, seeing a wonderful harmony in the Faith, finding no contradiction either within itself or with his own experience of life. Yet there can come moments in which it all feels like a dream, a totally coherent dream, but a dream. For most, the answer lies in Christ who was no dream, to whom revealed reality was no dream. His certainties can become ours, and the sense of dream vanishes.

That is the experience of many a Christian. What of Augustine? My own strong impression is that the sense of dream was not much apt to trouble him. We remember his two "luminous certainties." He was as little likely to question God's reality as his own. At the very beginning of this study of his praying, I suggested that there is far more sincerity, far more intensity anyhow, in our asking God for things than in our adoration. Again, I think not in Augustine's. He had discovered that man's way to God lies not in imagination, which is simply the soul's power to repicture what the body's senses have brought to it.

> My God was not yet You but the error and vain fantasy I held. When I tried to rest my burden upon them, I fell as through emptiness.

Slowly his intellect, helped by Plotinus, came to see God as spirit, beyond space, beyond time. And, helped by Paul, he saw

both the need of God's grace and what Christ had done to win grace for him. And it all built into a universe of which he was more certain than most men of the universe around them.

God was the atmosphere in which he was conscious of living, adoration the very breath of his life in it. He utters his adoration so frequently, that he must have been thinking and feeling it continuously. He lived in the excitement of God; yet he coped efficiently, tirelessly, with the unending dailiness of his duties as a bishop. Adoration meant seeing the glory of God, having seen his own total dependence on God, the total dependence in fact of everything on God. He could not see persons (himself among them) or things without in the same act seeing God holding them, all and each, in existence. It took him longer to see that whatever value was in them reflected the being of their Creator.

I I

You have made us for Yourself and our hearts are restless till they rest in You.

This is not only at the opening of the *Confessions,* it pervades them from end to end. It is not a mere piece of piety, the restlessness is a brute fact. Whatever is good, and therefore desirable, in anything whatsoever is there because God put it there, so that it must be in God—infinitely higher, but not less satisfying for that, not less desirable.

Those lovely things would be nothing at all unless they came from You.

In our weakness we may not lift ourselves to the level of actually desiring them as they are in God. But knowing that all things that attract us will be found in God in their totality, we know that there is no rest for us till we enter into possession of Him. And that will not be in this life.

"If anyone thinks that in this mortal life a man may so disperse the mists of bodily imaginings as to possess the unclouded light of changeless truth and cleave to it with the unswerving constancy of a spirit wholly estranged from the common ways of life—then he understands neither what he is searching for, nor himself who is making the search."

He had known the war in his members, the manifold tensions between the grace of God and a human nature not wholly yielded to God. He had learnt from Paul—perhaps in that study period for which he had asked his bishop—that they will not be brought to quiet here below.

Only in totally possessing God, which means being totally possessed by Him, shall restlessness be at an end. On earth only partial possession is possible.

I I I

Yet how great partial possession—with God's aid and our own willingness to be aided—can be.

Sometimes you admit me to a state of mind that I am not ordinarily in, a kind of delight which if it could ever be made permanent in us would be hard to distinguish from the life to come. But . . . I fall back again and am swallowed up by things customary.

Was this "state of mind" what has come to be called mystical union? Plotinus certainly had it, and the great Indian masters before him. Did Augustine? In *De Genesi ad Litteram* he speaks of "a transient intuition of God, accompanied by delight and spiritual sweetness." He says this in more detail (10.6). He lists things he especially loves in the created order—light and melody and fragrance and food and embrace. And he adds that all these he experiences in loving God—when "That light shines upon my soul which no space can contain, that voice sounds which no flowing away of time can take from me, I breathe that fragrance which no wind scatters, I eat the food which is not lessened by eating, and I lie in the embrace which satiety never comes to sunder. This is what I love when I love my God."

This passage contains echoes of Plotinus, and indeed Plotinus did set a mark upon Augustine's way of expressing himself—about a very different Absolute. But I cannot feel that he is describing the experience even of the Christian mystics who had absorbed Plotinus by way of the pseudo-Dionysius. There is too much "seeing," intuiting in Augustine's, theirs was all of touch and feeling with their intellect not in action, all its energy poured into the will.

I am no authority on Mysticism. My friend Edward Watkin has stated the opposite opinion, lucidly as always, in *A Monument to Saint Augustine*. For myself I feel that the intellect, inflamed by love, could produce every effect in the two passages I have quoted. Especially when the intellect is of the power of Augustine's.

> I shall mount beyond this my power of memory, I shall come to You, O Lovely Light. What have You to say to me? In my ascent by the mind to You, I shall mount up beyond that power of mind called

memory, longing to attain to touch You at the point where the contact is possible and to cleave to You at the point where it is possible to cleave.

IV

"Rare is the soul which, when it speaks of the Trinity, knows what it is saying" (13.11).

While he was writing the *Confessions,* Augustine was already working on the *De Trinitate,* "I was young when I began it, I finished it as an old man." Merely to gaze at it makes one realize why a fantastically busy bishop never found time for a full-length treatment of any other doctrine. Beyond any of the Fathers of the Church he made the Trinity *his* doctrine. So it is all the stranger that a legend about him is used on Trinity Sunday in sermons innumerable as a reason for preaching about something else.

On the improbable chance that this booklet of mine may fall into the hands of someone who has never heard the legend, here it is: Augustine was walking on a beach wrestling with the problem of the Three-in-One. He came upon a small boy who had dug a hole in the sand and was pouring sea-water into it.
Augustine: What are you doing?
Boy: I am trying to put the ocean into this hole.
Augustine: You can't get the whole vast ocean into that little hole.
Boy: And you can't get the whole vast ocean of the Trinity into your little head (or words to that effect). Whereupon the great saint decided to think about some other doctrine. Used, as the legend invariably is, as an excuse for not talking about the Trinity, it should

have been told about some other saint. His own sermons on the Trinity are a joy to read, especially Sermon 21 on "Blasphemy against the Holy Spirit" and Sermon 139 on "I and the Father are one." And, sermons apart, no one in the Western World had—or has to this day without his assistance—written as deeply and clearly and at such length on it as Augustine—"I was young when I began it, I finished it as an old man."

For being tormented because we cannot know God as well as He knows Himself, Augustine was an even worse choice. He was too intelligent to be irked at not being omniscient. Thinking on the Trinity must have its proportion of toil and sweat and anguished longing for more light, but I think he got more mental delight than anguish out of it. Had it been predestination, perhaps. . . .

I can remember only one prayer explicitly directed to Father, Son and Holy Spirit in the *Confessions,* which as I have said he was still writing when he began the *De Trinitate*. Apparently the God of whom he was so luminously certain took on this new light without its needing extra identification in prayer. The word "God" still said everything to him. He could not say it without having the Father present to him—Son and Holy Spirit not dividing the Oneness but enriching it, with their reminder that in the Godhead knowledge is not something but Someone, love not something but Someone.

> Holy, Holy, Holy, O Lord my God: in Your name were we baptized, O Father, Son and Holy Spirit, in Your name do we baptize, O Father, Son and Holy Spirit.

THE PRAYER OF LOVE

Late have I loved You, O Beauty so ancient and so new. Late have I loved You! For behold You were within me and I was outside; and I sought You outside, and in my unloveliness fell upon those lovely things which You have made.

I

Our quotations under Adoration contain Love in equal measure. And in Augustine they had become inseparable.

In his commentary on John 5:7 he writes, "The only thing that distinguishes the children of God from the children of the devil is love." A little later in the same Commentary we find another of his very famous phrases, usually quoted as *Ama et fac quod vis*. We think of it along with "Give what You command, then command what You will," a prayer which infuriated Pelagius with its flat contradiction of his own "God made us human, we make ourselves righteous." And indeed Augustine's phrase does not escape the danger which lies in wait for all epigrams—that too much is omitted for the sake of streamlining: it calls for a half-page of interpretation. All the same, in its streamlined compactness it has been a creative explosion.

I I

You do not enquire too fiercely into our sins.

As we have seen, he assumes that, if he had died of a near-fatal illness before his conversion, he would have been lost eternally.

How Augustine reconciles God as loving men and wanting their love with God as inflicting punishment, he does not tell us. I have not studied this question over the whole of his writing; but in the *Confessions* at least, while he is sure that God scourges us for our healing, I feel that he sees damnation as resulting not from the demands of God's justice but from man's refusal to love. Refusal to love is what makes life with God in heaven impossible: in a Sermon quoted earlier, he uses the phrase about hatred—"something has died in us." We cannot enter life with love dead in us.

"The merciful shall obtain mercy," he reminds us. Evidently he is thinking of sinners who need mercy, otherwise the question of their obtaining it would not arise. They do obtain it—because they have been merciful. It is the meaning of Paul's "charity covers a multitude of sins," of "forgive us our debts as we forgive our debtors." Charity, willingness to forgive, mercy—all three mean that love is not dead; and love, even a spark of love, cannot go down to eternal loss.

I I I

What does it mean to love God? Most of us find that our experience of loving people—the emotional stirring, the pleasure in being with them, even (if we have it) the willingness to make sacrifices for them, above all the sense of a contact in depth—none of these is easily translated into our relation to God. With Augustine, as we have just heard, they all were—to the point where he could almost have reversed St. John's, "If we do not love men whom we have seen, how shall we love God, whom we have not seen?"

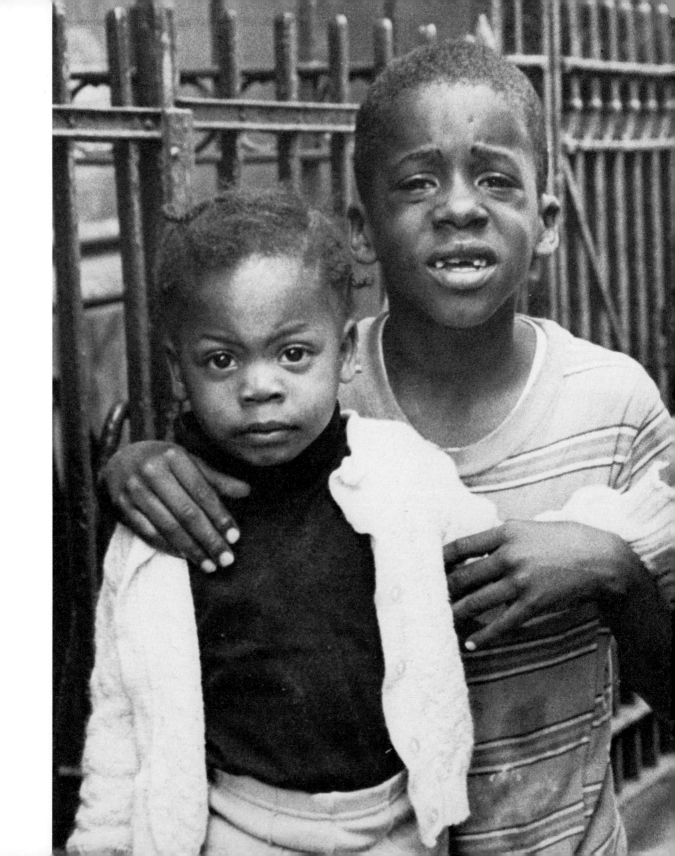

That he could reach this level of love we have seen. Could he remain fixed in it? He has told us that he could not. We have heard his wistful "If only it could be permanent." I do not know who first said to God *"Concupivi desiderare Te"*—Augustine perhaps. It can be translated roughly as "I have longed to yearn for You." Augustine must sometimes have felt just that longing for a yearning he could not manage to attain—not as often as most devout souls feel it perhaps. Yet even of that one cannot be sure. The longings and the yearnings experienced by most of us are pallid compared with the passionateness of his. A yearning for God which might seem to you and me very close to mystical union might have seemed to him hardly worth offering to God.

We remember how Aquinas towards the end said "All I have written is straw." Augustine had the same feeling:

> With all this what have I said my God and my life and my delight? What can anyone say when he talks of You?

He was not pretending when he wrote that, nor when, early in the *Confessions,* he writes:

> Hear me as I pray, O Lord . . . that I should find more delight in You than in all the temptations I once ran after, and should love You more intensely and cling to Your hand with all my heart's strength, and be delivered from every temptation unto the end

—a prayer that may seem less remote from the reality of ourselves after we have travelled Augustine's road with him.

No, he felt he should have uttered God better, should have fought temptation better, should have returned God's love better:

Give Yourself to me, O my God, give Yourself once more to me. I love You and if my love is too small a thing grant me to love more intensely. I cannot measure to know how far my love falls short of sufficiency, that my life should run to Your embrace and never be turned away until it is hidden in the secret of Your face (13.9).